Greater Than a Tour

I think the series is wonderful and beneficial for tourists to get information before visiting the city.
-Seckin Zumbul, Izmir Turkey

I am a world traveler who has read many trip guides but this one really made a difference for me. I would call it a heartfelt creation of a local guide expert instead of just a guide.
-Susy, Isla Holbox, Mexico

New to the area like me, this is a must have!
-Joe, Bloomington, USA

This is a good series that gets down to it when looking for things to do at your destination without having to read a novel for just a few ideas.
-Rachel, Monterey, USA

Good information to have to plan my trip to this destination.
-Pennie Farrell, Mexico

Aptly titled, you won't just be a tourist after reading this book. You'll be greater than a tourist!
-Alan Warner, Grand Rapids, USA

Thank you for a fantastic book.
-Don, Philadelphia, USA

John Smither

Great ideas for a port day.
-Mary Martin USA

Even though I only have three days to spend in San Miguel in an upcoming visit, I will use the author's suggestions to guide some of my time there. An easy read - with chapters named to guide me in directions I want to go.
-Robert Catapano, USA

Great insights from a local perspective! Useful information and a very good value!
-Sarah, USA

This series provides an in-depth experience through the eyes of a local. Reading these series will help you to travel the city in with confidence and it'll make your journey a unique one.
-Andrew Teoh, Ipoh, Malaysia

Tourists can get an amazing "insider scoop" about a lot of places from all over the world. While reading, you can feel how much love the writer put in it.
-Vanja Živković, Sremski Karlovci, Serbia

>TOURIST

GREATER THAN A TOURIST – CHENGDU SICHUAN PROVINCE CHINA

50 Travel Tips from a Local

John Smither

John Smither

Greater Than a Tourist- Chengdu Sichuan Province China Copyright © 2018 by CZYK Publishing LLC.
All Rights Reserved.

All rights reserved. No part of this book may be reproduced in any form or by any electronic or mechanical means including information storage and retrieval systems, without permission in writing from the author. The only exception is by a reviewer, who may quote short excerpts in a review.

Cover designed by Ivana Stamenković
Cover images: https://pixabay.com/en/chengdu-the-scenery-tourism-sichuan-1739804/
https://pixabay.com/en/kazakhstan-astana-1886796/

Greater Than a Tourist
Visit our website at www.GreaterThanaTourist.com

Lock Haven, PA
All rights reserved.

ISBN: 9781980602149

>TOURIST

50 TRAVEL TIPS FROM A LOCAL

John Smither

BOOK DESCRIPTION

Are you excited about planning your next trip?
Do you want to try something new?
Would you like some guidance from a local?

If you answered yes to any of these questions, then this Greater Than a Tourist book is for you.

Greater Than a Tourist- Chengdu Sichuan Province China by John Smither offers the inside scoop on Chengdu. Most travel books tell you how to travel like a tourist. Although there is nothing wrong with that, as part of the Greater Than a Tourist series, this book will give you travel tips from someone who has lived at your next travel destination.

In these pages, you will discover advice that will help you throughout your stay. This book will not tell you exact addresses or store hours but instead will give you excitement and knowledge from a local that you may not find in other smaller print travel books.

Travel like a local. Slow down, stay in one place, and get to know the people and the culture. By the time you finish this book, you will be eager and prepared to travel to your next destination.

John Smither

TABLE OF CONTENTS

BOOK DESCRIPTION
TABLE OF CONTENTS
DEDICATION
ABOUT THE AUTHOR
HOW TO USE THIS BOOK
FROM THE PUBLISHER
OUR STORY
WELCOME TO
> TOURIST
INTRODUCTION
1. Come To Chengdu To See Giant Pandas
2. An Ancient Irrigation System
3. Chengdu Metro
4. Railway Stations
5. Chengdu Shuangliu International Airport
6. Baoguang Temple
7. Chengdu Botanical Garden
8. Chengdu Museum
9. Hotels In Chengdu
10. Chengdu's Hostel Choices
11. A Day At The Zoo
12. Chunxi Road
13. Dinosaur Museum
14. Polar Ocean World
15. Happy Valley
16. Huanglong National Scenic Reserve

John Smither

17. Huanglongxi Ancient Town
19. Jinli Street
20. Jinsha Site Museum
21. Jiuyanqiao Bar Street
22. Luodai Ancient Town
23. Food Tours
24. Walking Tours
25. Half Day Bike Tour
26. Mount Qingcheng
27. People's Park
28. Pingle Ancient Town
29. Qingyang Palace
30. History Of The Salt Industry Museum
31. Stone Elephant Lake
32. Sichuan Cuisine Museum
33. Thatched Cottage Of Du Fu
34. Sichuan Museum
35. Tianfu Square
36. Sichuan Museum of Science and Technology
37. Wangjiang Pavilion Park
38. Wenshu Monastery
39. Wide and Narrow Alley
40. Wuhou Temple
41. Xiling Snow Mountain
42. Yongling Museum
43. Zhaojue Temple
44. Leshan Giant Buddha
45. Mount Emei
46. Jiayang Steam Train

47. Sichuan Opera
48. Shopping
49. Anshun Bridge
50. Wenshufang Folk and Culture Street
> TOURIST
GREATER THAN A TOURIST
> TOURIST
GREATER THAN A TOURIST
NOTES

DEDICATION

This book is dedicated to Sichuan's people and not just those in the province's capital of Chengdu for the warmth and friendship they have shown me over several years, Thank you.

John Smither

ABOUT THE AUTHOR

John Smither is a freelance writer and teacher from the UK who first arrived in Chengdu in early 2008 after a 44 hour train journey from Beijing. In total he has lived in Sichuan for 4 years and enjoyed his free time in Chengdu.

I feel very lucky to have led the life I have had, to travel the world and see so many places, my travel experiences have been mostly through working abroad and then relishing each new place and learning all I can about that location whilst I am there.

John Smither

HOW TO USE THIS BOOK

The Greater Than a Tourist book series was written by someone who has lived in an area for over three months. The goal of this book is to help travelers either dream or experience different locations by providing opinions from a local. The author has made suggestions based on their own experiences. Please do your own research before traveling to the area in case the suggested places are unavailable.

John Smither

FROM THE PUBLISHER

Traveling can be one of the most important parts of a person's life. The anticipation and memories that you have are some of the best. As a publisher of the Greater Than a Tourist book series, as well as the popular 50 Things to Know book series, we strive to help you learn about new places, spark your imagination, and inspire you. Wherever you are and whatever you do I wish you safe, fun, and inspiring travel.

Lisa Rusczyk Ed. D.
CZYK Publishing

John Smither

OUR STORY

Traveling is a passion of the "Greater than a Tourist" series creator. Lisa studied abroad in college, and for their honeymoon Lisa and her husband toured Europe. During her travels to Malta, an older man tried to give her some advice based on his own experience living on the island since he was a young boy. She was not sure if she should talk to the stranger but was interested in his advice. When traveling to some places she was wary to talk to locals because she was afraid that they weren't being genuine. Through her travels, Lisa learned how much locals had to share with tourists. Lisa created the "Greater Than a Tourist" book series to help connect people with locals. A topic that locals are very passionate about sharing.

John Smither

WELCOME TO
> TOURIST

John Smither

INTRODUCTION

"A mind that is stretched by a new experience can never go back to its old dimensions."
–Oliver Wendell Holmes

For me, the new experience I found in Sichuan was that of the spicy food. Genuine Sichuan food is at a level of spicy that I had not previously encountered, it was off the scale. If you like spicy food you will love spicy, even if I asked for non spicy food it would be a little spicy.

Another new experience for me in Sichuan was earthquakes, before 2008 there had not been a major earthquake in the province for over 70 years. Within 3 months of my arrival they had a big one. Over the next four or 5 years there were regular rumblings of the ground. I moved on from Sichuan in 2013, since then it has been free of earthquakes, some of my Chinese friends jokingly suggest I stay away.

Here are 50 things, greater than a tourist to do in Chengdu, the capital city of Sichuan province.

John Smither

>TOURIST

1. Come To Chengdu To See Giant Pandas

The Giant Panda Research Base is just 10km from the city centre and is the most conveniently located panda centre to visit. Giant Pandas are only found in Sichuan Gansu and Shaanxi provinces with fewer than 2000 left in the wild. Over 70% of the panda population is in Sichuan and it is through the dedication of centres like this that the panda population is slowly increasing in size. It is a wonderful setting and I love to visit here whenever I return to the city. In addition to the giant pandas there are red pandas, cranes, storks and another 20 species of animals that are endangered in the wild.

To visit the Panda Centre take the metro line 3 to Panda Avenue, then a shuttle bus will take you to the entrance. The entry fee is CNY58 and it is open daily from 7.30am until 6pm. the best time to visit is from 9am until 10am during breakfast feeding time.

2. An Ancient Irrigation System

Dujiangyan Irrigation System is a simple but effective flood control system devised more than 2200 years ago. It provides an irrigation system as well as preventing floods to over 50 cities in Sichuan province. This irrigation system is the world's oldest and only surviving non-dam system of flood and irrigation control, it has been hailed as a wonder of Chinese science. The best place to view this project is from the Anlan Cable Bridge; the original bridge was constructed before the Song Dynasty of 960-1279 and made of wooden blocks and bamboo. The bridge today is constructed of steel and concrete. Other historical attractions here include the Fulong Temple.

To visit the Dujiangyan Scenic Area you can take a fast train from Chengdu to be in Dujiangyan city in 30 minutes then take a tourist bus, or tale a bus from Chengdu directly to the scenic area. The entry fee is CNY90 and it is open daily from 8am until 6pm (5.30pm in the winter).

3. Chengdu Metro

Chengdu's metro system opened in 2010 and currently has six lines in operation with 138 stations on its 180km of tracks. By 2020 there will be almost 300km of lines open which will eventually be extended to over 400km on 21 lines. Line 10 opened to Chengdu airport in 2017 making the journey into the city much easier than it had been. It is a very clean mode of transport and English is widely used throughout the network from purchasing tickets to train information and announcements, this makes it a very good and convenient choice of travel for non Chinese speaking visitors.

4. Railway Stations

There are currently three railway stations in Chengdu, Chengdu South has limited services after opening in 2014, Changdu East handles most of the high speed trains in and out of the city and opened in 2011. The oldest station Chengdu Railway Station is in the north of the city and can be a little confusing. Beneath the railway station is a metro station and it is called Chengdu North, many locals refer to the station as the north station but there is in fact a Chengdu North station, 17km further to the north on the second ring road but it is a freight yard and not a passenger station. Chengdu is one of the major railway hubs in China with direct connections to most major cities in China.

5. Chengdu Shuangliu International Airport

Chengdu's international airport is located 16km to the southwest of the city centre and is the fourth busiest airport in China and the most important in the south west of the country. It has flights from 170 destinations from within China and more than 50 international destinations worldwide. Transportation from the airport is very good with the metro, shuttle buses and taxis into the city centre giving plenty of options. There is also a station for high speed trains at the airport with regular trains from the city centre to Emeishan and Leshan scenic areas further to the south.

6. Baoguang Temple

This ancient Buddhist temple is 18km to the north of the city centre with some splendid structures to make your visit a pleasant one with many locals believing that praying here will ensure your wishes come true. Walking across the square you will see a screen wall, inscribed in the wall is the Chinese character for good luck or good fortune. You may observe groups of Chinese people waiting their turn to touch this symbol. There is a set way this must be done, with your eyes closed and walking from a distance, if you connect directly with the symbol you will have good fortune in the coming year. The next attraction you will see is a leaning stupa, it is a 13 storey elaborate and magnificent structure built during the Tang dynasty of 618-907. There are the remains of 13 Buddha's kept inside the stupa.

 The entry fee is CNY5 and it is open daily from 8am until 5pm, you can take bus number 651 to Baoguangsi Station, there are other options but this is probably the easiest one. About two hours is the recommended time to allow for a visit.

7. Chengdu Botanical Garden

 This attraction is a great place for relaxing away from the busy city life; it is about 10km north of the centre of the city and has over 2000 plant species, 1000 species of woody plants and 800 varieties of horticultural plants. In the area of the flower gardens there is a flower show held every year from early March until early in April, this is one of the best times of year to visit here. The recreation area is full of stone trails which wind their way through the tall trees offering shelter from the sun and occasionally the wind. You can buy some food and relax in the many areas set aside for this purpose, it is a popular area for flying kites, drinking tea and playing mahjong.

 There are several bus routes that go to the botanical garden, the entrance fee is just CNY10 and it is open from 6.30am until 8pm in June until August, the rest of the year it opens from 7am until 7pm.

8. Chengdu Museum

This museum is located in the city centre to the west of Tianfu Square. It is the biggest museum in the city consisting of two towers although only one is open to the public. There are six floors with the basement and first floor used for temporary exhibitions. The history of Chengdu is shown on the second through to the fourth floors. The fifth floor has demonstrations and exhibits on the arts of puppetry and shadow play. The history of Chengdu is shown from the Qin Dynasty of 211-206BC with over 240 relics on display through to the Qing dynasty that ended in 1911. The exhibits include water transportation methods, the flourishing market culture as well as local handicrafts. You can get a taste of the 20th century and modern Chengdu on the fourth floor of the museum with local folk customs playing an important role in local Sichuan life.

The easiest way to reach this museum is on the metro, take lines 1 or 2 to the Tianfu Square station and walk across the square to the west, the museum entrance is in front of you. Entry to the museum is free although you must show your ID, such as a passport to enter. It is closed on Mondays, every other day it opens at 9am and closes at 8.30pm from May until October, the rest of the year it closes at 8pm.

9. Hotels In Chengdu

There are hundreds of hotels across the city suitable for all with budget hotels available from just CNY100 per night even in the city centre. Mid range hotels are generally in the price range of CNY300-700, although you can find some good deals online out of the high season so it is worth having a look for bargains. Most hotels in this category will have one or two of their staff that speak some English at least at a basic level. You do usually get a free Chinese style breakfast included in the price of your room although most Chinese breakfasts are not popular with overseas visitors.

The luxury hotel market in Chengdu is very reasonably priced and out of season you can get some real bargains on your accommodation choices. You should find fluency in their English speaking staff so communication is not a problem. They will have western style restaurants with familiar food options in addition to Chinese. You should expect to pay anything from CNY750 to well over CNY1000 per room per night, but cheaper deals can be found online if you shop around.

10. Chengdu's Hostel Choices

Chengdu has a great selection of international hostels with more than 15 hostels that are highly rated with knowledgeable English speaking staff and plenty to offer those travelers on a lower budget. I can personally recommend the Mix Hostel, it is close to the Wenshu monastery with dorm rooms from CNY60 and private en-suite rooms from CNY200 per night. They offer free walking tours of the local area as well as assist you in booking tours to the major attractions you will wish to see.

11. A Day At The Zoo

Chengdu's Zoo is the largest in the southwest of China with over 300 species of animals among the 3000 on show. You can see Giant Pandas, Leopards, South China Tigers and so much more. There are 16 different areas or houses including the monkey house, the panda house where 58 pandas have been bred and raised and the lion, tiger and leopard house where you can closely observe the big cats. The zoo is to be found on the South Zhaojuesi Road in the district of Chenghua, you can easily reach the zoo on metro line 3 or several bus routes go there. Get off at the zoo station, Dong Wu Yuan and enter by the north gate nearby. The zoo costs CNY20 and is open daily from 8am until 5pm.

12. Chunxi Road

Is the centre of fashion in Chengdu, connecting the commercial centres of East Street and the Mercantile Corporation, as well as fashion it is also famous as a place for getting great tasting street food. Part way along the street is a granite wall with eight scenes from the Tang dynasty of 609-917. Further down the street is a statue of Sun Yat-sen in Yat-sen Square, it is a good place to sit and rest. Around this square are several sculptures each depicting Chengdu's culture and history. Inside the shopping centre there are more than 700 stores of all sizes selling more than just fashionable items. If you are hungry there are lots of local snacks available from the kiosks and stalls around this area. You can take lines 2 or 3 of Chengdu metro to get here and leave by exit C or D. there are also several bus routes that converge here. Most stores open at 10am and close at 10pm, every day.

13. Dinosaur Museum

One of the world's biggest dinosaur museum's can be found at Zigong a couple of hours to the south of Chengdu. Since it opened in 1987 the museum has been held in high regard as a world leader in its field with life like exhibits, fossils and plant information during the age of these creatures in addition to rare dinosaurs. The museum is in three sections, the first giving you an introduction to these ancient creatures. The second part of the exhibition is showing the fossils that have been found locally as well as recreated life-size models of some species of dinosaurs. The final part of the museum shows where these ancient creatures were buried more than 100 million years ago. Several bus stations operate buses from Chengdu to Zigong, and then take a local bus number 35 to the site of the museum. It costs CNY40 to enter and is open daily from 8.30am until 5pm.

14. Polar Ocean World

This interesting attraction is located at the southern end of Tianfu Avenue in Chengdu. It has performances by dolphins, sea lions and whales among others and attracts many visitors. The animals are well trained to interact with people to get the reward of a fish. Other animals in the exhibition area and not performing include sharks and turtles, from the dangerous to the majestic. You can then go and see the penguins as they dive en-masse into the water or the polar bears as they show why they are one of the most feared animals close to the

North Pole. There are lots of bus routes that operate here; there are currently no metro lines close by although line 1 will pass here when the extension is opened. The entry fee is CNY190 and it is open daily from 9am until 6pm.

15. Happy Valley

The Happy Valley theme park in Jinniu district of Chengdu is 7km to the north west of the city centre and opened in 2009 as the third theme park in China under the Happy Valley logo. There are currently 6 roller coasters at the park with the last two being added in 2016. There are in total more than 130 rides and other smaller attractions at the theme park. The Ferris wheel gives you amazing views over the park and beyond. There is a 4-D cinema so it feels like you are in the movie and not just watching, if that isn't exciting enough why not try bungee jumping?

Several bus routes go to the Happy Valley theme park, a ticket that gives you unlimited access to all the rides costs CNY230. The night ticket valid from 6pm until 10pm costs CNY100.

16. Huanglong National Scenic Reserve

Huanglong meaning "Yellow Dragon" is the name given to this scenic area in North West Sichuan of colourful lakes, snow clad mountains and forest. The valley is said to resemble a dragon as it winds its way through the forest. The numerous lakes are strewn with limestone deposits that are coloured gold; in the sunlight the shimmering water moves like a dragon. The area has lots of caves, waterfalls and springs. Feicui Spring is among the ten most famous in China and brings medicinal value through the water. The average annual temperature is a cool 7C, with misty mornings and evenings. There is a lot of rainfall every year from May until August. The admission fee from May until November is CNY200, the rest of the year it is just CNY60. It is open daily from 8am until 5pm.

17. Huanglongxi Ancient Town

this ancient town is in Shuangliu county to the south east of Chengdu, it has a history of over 1700 years and is full of beautiful scenery and ancient culture. Chengdu was the capital of the Shu Kingdom in the Three kingdoms Period of 220-280AD, at that time Huanglongxi was of great military importance. Seven ancient streets are well preserved as are three ancient temples along Central Street. It is an important centre for archaeological research and the ancient streets are often used by movie makers, the location has appeared on more than 100 Chinese movies and TV shows. The ancient town is free to visit; you can take a bus here from Xinnanmen Bus Station in Chengdu costing CNY15 or 16 each way.

18. Huanhua Stream Park

This park also known as Huanhuaxi Park is the largest urban forest park in Chengdu. It is located between the first and second ring roads with the Sichuan Museum to its eastern side and the Thatched Cottage of Du Fu located to the north. It is a natural link between these two major attractions of Chengdu. The pleasant natural scenery together with the wetland areas of the park make this green space a favourite location for locals to relax away from the busy streets. Some of the major features include Canglang Lake, Egret Island and Poetry Avenue that leads the way up to the Thatched Cottage. It is 388 metres long with more than 300 statues of ancient Chinese poets lined up on either side. There are lots of buses that pass by this park, entry to the park is free and it is open daily from 6am until 10pm.

19. Jinli Street

Jinli Street can be found to the east of Wuhou Temple, since the Qin dynasty of 221BC-206BC, this street has been famous for its rich ornate cloth. It was in the centre of the commercial district during the Shu Kingdom, then known as the First Street of the Shu. After restoration work it was reopened to the public in 2004, since then visitors have gathered here to shop, relax and admire the traditional style buildings. Jinli Street of today begins under an imposing archway and extends for 350 metres with cultural buildings housing tea shops, hotels and stores all built in the style of the Qing dynasty.

As you stroll along this street take a look at some of the local crafts on display not just inside the stores but also at the stalls that set up each morning. In the centre of the street is a small stage, occasionally it will be used to perform Sichuan opera, if you are able to see one of these shows you will be amazed.

20. Jinsha Site Museum

This ancient site was only discovered in 2001 and the museum is designed to protect and study further the archaeological findings of this valuable site. The site dates to around 3000 years ago from the Shang Dynasty that ruled from the 17th until the 11th century BC. The area covers about 5 square kilometers and consists of 63 sacrificial spots, over 70 buildings, 3 cemeteries and 6000 precious relics. Unearthed has been the most concentrated collection in the world of ancient ivory and elephant skulls and teeth.

The collection of gold articles is the most found in China from this period in history, in addition to this is the biggest collection of Jade of the Bronze Age. Over 2000 pieces of Jade have been discovered most would have been used in sacrificial ceremonies. The easiest way to visit this wonderful site is on the metro, take line 7 to the Jinsha Yizhi. The entry fee is CNY80, it is closed on Mondays except for Mondays during January, February, July and August and when a public holiday falls on a Monday. It is open from 8am until 8pm from March until October, 8am until 6.30pm from November until April.

21. Jiuyanqiao Bar Street

This famous bar street in the Jinjiang district is next to the Jinjiang River and is renowned for its diversity of bars. Some are peaceful where you can sit and chat, others are very lively and deafening. If you prefer somewhere quiet you should try SOHO Bar, 88 Bar, White Night, 1855 or Bund No.1 Bar. All of these bars are small and great places to just sit and talk about your day with some friends. 1855 is a favourite haunt of students with cheap priced drinks while White Night is owned by a poet and the bar is full of books and art.

If you prefer bars that are playing lively exciting and loud music then try places such as Muse, Zero Bar or Le Petit Bar. They give opportunities to local bands to perform, the quality may not always be the best but they are great locations to release your energy after a hard and stressful day at work.

22. Luodai Ancient Town

This ancient town is just 18km from the centre of Chengdu and is home to the Hakka people, a small ethnic minority that makes up 90% of the local population of over 20,000. The town has a long history dating back to the Three Kingdoms Period that existed from 220-280AD. The buildings and local culture are well preserved here and it is easy to immerse yourself into this culture. The area around the old street is one main street 1200 metres in length and crossed by seven lanes.

There are four guild halls in the ancient town all erected during the Qing dynasty with exquisite detail in their painting and carving. The most famous of these four halls is Guangdong Hall, also known as Nanhua Palace it was built in 1746 and it is one of the largest and best preserved guild halls in China.

The Hakka Museum is a testament to their people, it tells of their migration to Sichuan, displays the cultural relics and crafts of the Hakka. In the Hakka Park you will find tea houses, one of them is a women's teahouse, it was traditionally forbidden for Hakka men to enter. The easiest way to get here from Chengdu is to take the bus directly from Xinanmen Bus Station to the Ancient Town. The Ancient Town is free to enter and is open all day, every day.

John Smither

23. Food Tours

There are several operators of culinary tours of the city and most hotels or hostels can provide you with details. The style of cuisine in Sichuan has been developed over centuries. It has a distinct flavour with its piquant spicy taste. Typical local dishes include Ma Po Tofu, this is to be found in just about every restaurant in Sichuan, it is bean curd with mince and chili oil and one of the best restaurants for this is Chen Ma Po's Bean Curd Restaurant on West Yulong Street.

One of my favourites is Kung Pao Chicken; it is made from diced spicy chicken with peanuts and a Sichuan delicacy. Fish Flavoured Shredded Pork is made up of shredded pork, carrots and bamboo shoots; it contains no fish, just the flavour. You can find these dishes all over Chengdu, the best choices of restaurants are close to Tianfu Square. All over the city you can find stalls selling street food, from meat or fish skewers to sausages and glutinous rice balls. All the snack foods are very cheap at less than CNY5.

24. Walking Tours

Most of the international hostels in Chengdu offer their guests a walking tour of the city; many of these are free and usually end at a tea house. They are a great way to learn about the city, good places to eat and what attractions there are to see from a local. You will often learn something on these tours that are not listed in the guide books; it is an interesting way to spend a morning or afternoon.

25. Half Day Bike Tour

Another half day tour you can thoroughly enjoy and use up a little more energy is on a bike or cycling tour of the city. The cost is around CNY230 and includes the bike as well as an English speaking guide. You will be taken to landmarks such as the Wenshu Monastery, Qingyang Palace and the People's Park. The pace of the ride is set by your ability on the bike, but the emphasis is on a relaxing and leisurely ride.

26. Mount Qingcheng

This sacred mountain is one of the most famous mountains devoted to Taoism in China; it is in an area of Sichuan close to Dijiangyan, surrounded by neighbouring peaks in a secluded evergreen setting. The mountain setting covers an area of 15 square kilometers and includes Jianfu Palace which was originally built in the Tang dynasty between 618 and 907. Shanqing Palace is where you can pay homage to the supreme deities in Taoism through the stone statues of Huangdi, Shennong and Fuxi. They are the Three Sovereigns of ancient China.

Tianshi Cave is the most important temple on the mountain, inside is a statue of Zhang Tianshi who preached here during the Eastern Han Dynasty of 25-220AD. Zhang Tianshi is regarded as the founder of Taoism on this mountain. At its highest point on the peak of the mountain you will find Laojun Pavilion. To visit here you can take a high speed train from Chengdu to Qingchengshan, then bus 101 to the mountain. The cost is split into different areas; the front mountain with most of the attractions is CNY90, while the rear mountain costs CNY20. There are cable cars costing from CNY35-80, while you can go boating from CNY2-5.

27. People's Park

The People's Park is close to Tianfu Square on Shaocheng Road. It was built in 1911 and is a favourite location for local people to relax, drink tea, dance or play mahjong. There are many famous spots within the park including Rockery Square, it is close to the East Gate and built in 2004 using 3000 tons of rocks to create a hill from which a fascinating waterfall now descends. Goldfish Island is surrounded by a lake that is home to hundreds of goldfish; on the island is one of several teahouses in the park where you can watch the entertainment of local performers. In the north west of the park you will find the Memorial to the Railway Protection Movement. This memorial is dedicated to the people that sacrificed themselves during the struggle in 1911 against the private construction of railways being sold to foreign companies. There are several flower gardens to observe around the park as well as a children's playground close to the south gate. To get to the park there are several bus routes to the nearby Tianfu Square or you can take the Metro line 2, to the People's Park station. Use exit B and walk to the north gate of the park. It is free to enter the park and is open daily from 6.30am until 10pm.

28. Pingle Ancient Town

This historical town is full of ancient culture in Qionglai City 65km to the south west of Chengdu with a history going back over 2000 years. It sits on the Baimo River and has stilt houses built in the traditional style and banyan trees over 1000 years old. There are 22 ancient streets leading away from the ancient wharf with traditional two storey houses where the lower floor is used for storage and the upper floor for living.

There has been a dam here since the time of Yu the Great, the first emperor of the Xia dynasty from the 21st-17th centuries BC, this structure has prevented flooding since that time. There are also ancient temples and Guanyin Bodhisatta Monastery houses the Moya Great Buddha dating from the Tang dynasty of 618-907.Leshan Bridge is the largest ancient stone bridge in Sichuan it was constructed in 1861 and measures 120 metres long. One of the ancient crafts is paper, there are 74 sites of paper workshops dating from the Southern Song dynasty of 1127-1279 in this ancient town. Another historical relic from this location is an ancient post road. It was part of the Southern Silk Road dating from the Qin Dynasty of 221-207BC, the section in the ancient town is well preserved. There are several other attractions in the area including rock climbing and a cable bridge. There are five buses that leave Xinanmen bus station in Chengdu each day for the two hour journey to this site, the fare is CNY33. Entry into the ancient town is free, although you will have to pay individually for some attractions.

29. Qingyang Palace

This palace is in fact a Taoist temple and one of the most famous in Chengdu; it is located in the north west of the city and dates from the Tang dynasty of 618-907. Most of what you see today is reconstructions dating from the Qing dynasty of 1644-1911. Standing beside the altar in Sanqing Hall are two bronze goats. One of the goats has a mouse's ears, a tiger's claw, and an ox's nose. It is actually made up of the features of the 12 animals used in the Chinese zodiac. Lots of local people spend their free time here drinking tea, playing mahjong or just relaxing. The entry fee is CNY10 and you should allow an hour for a visit.

30. History Of The Salt Industry Museum

This museum in the city of Zigong is the only salt museum in China and since its inauguration in 1959 it has been its intention to study, collect, preserve and put on display the implements related to the industry of salt mining. There are more than 1300 exhibits including a complete set of 500 drilling tools that help to tell the story of this 2000 year old industry. Part of the interactive experience of the museum allows visitors to operate some of the machinery. You can take a bus from Chengdu direct to the salt museum the entry fee is CNY20 and it is open all year from 8.30am until 5.30pm.

31. Stone Elephant Lake

Also known as Shixiang Lake, it is to be found 89km south west of Chengdu and is named after the Stone Elephant Temple which is beside the lake. Walking beside the lake is a maze of turnings as you enter numerous small bays. The temple was erected during the Three Kingdoms Period of 220-280AD and contains a Jade Buddha Hall among the 6 halls you can view. Tourists are able to row boats on the lake and surrounded by forests it is easy to become lost among the natural beauty of the scenery. The trees of the forest are 90% Chinese Red Pines, these trees give off a high content of oxygen so walking among the trees can be very beneficial to your lungs and heart.

Buses depart from Xinnanmen bus station in Chengdu each morning at 9am, 10am and 10.20am for the 90 minute journey to the Elephant Lake and the fare is CNY33. Entry to the temple and lake area is CNY80. Rowing on the lake costs CNY40 and the attraction is open daily from 8.30am until 5.30pm.

32. Sichuan Cuisine Museum

This is the world's only museum dedicated to the culture of Sichuan cuisine; it is located in Pidu 33km north west of Chengdu. The museum contains books, recipes, raw materials, pictures and the utensils required to create Sichuan's cuisine. During a tour of the museum you are invited to taste some of the local foods on display. The museum has an exhibition hall, an interactive hall, a kitchen temple and a raw materials hall. The exhibition hall holds over 3000 items used in cooking with some exhibits used during the Warring States Period of 475-221BC. In the raw material hall there are 200 pots of chili paste, a key ingredient in Sichuan cooking. Visitors are encouraged to make some themselves. You can try to make your own dish under the supervision of a chef in the interactive area. The museum is open daily from 9am until 6pm. there is a CNY60 entry fee for this museum, CNY360 to take part in the cooking activities.

33. Thatched Cottage Of Du Fu

This popular attraction is 5km to the south west of Tianfu Square and was the poet Du Fu's home during the Tang dynasty. Du Fu was born in Henan province in 712, he fled the An-Shi rebellion in what is today Xian in 758 and arrived in Chengdu the following year. His cottage was built on the outskirts of the city and during the next four years he wrote over 240 poems that today are considered to be national treasures.

The cottage was abandoned for centuries and reconstructed in 1500 and 1811; these set the basis for the cottage today. You can visit the cottage by taking metro line 4 to North Caotong Road Station and walking for about 15 minutes or alternatively several bus routes pass by the entrance. The entry fee is CNY60 and it is open from 8am until 8pm (6.30pm from October until April).

34. Sichuan Museum

The Sichuan Museum is located in the west of Chengdu and next to Huanhua Stream Park. It is south western China's largest comprehensive museum. There are 14 exhibition halls across the three floors of the museum hosting a variety of unique exhibits in the 260,000 items on display. The first floor area is a multifunctional reception area that includes pottery exhibits from the Han Dynasty of 202BC until 220AD. On the second floor there is a collection of Bronze Ware dating from the States of Ba and Shu (Shu was the original name given to what is today Sichuan), it also contains paintings, calligraphy and fine ceramics. The third floor is where you will find relics to Tibetan Buddhism, cultural relics to Sichuan ethnicity including folk art and crafts.

You can use metro lines 2 and 4 to reach the museum; exit at the University of TCM Station via exit A, it is then a ten minute walk to the museum entrance. It is free entry to the museum with your ID or a passport, you should note only 4000 free tickets are issued each day. The museum is closed on Mondays and is open from 9am until 5pm. On Saturday's it remains open until 8pm.

35. Tianfu Square

Tianfu Square is one of the focal points of Chengdu and located in the heart of the city centre. It is the largest city square to be found in the south west of China. Metro lines 1 and 2 meet below the square and it is an important meeting place in the heart of the business and commercial district. It is an open space where you can leisurely enjoy the trees and flowers while surrounded by the skyscrapers of the modern city. In the evening the fountains are illuminated and a musical display entertains tourists and locals with this free aquatic show.

There are several attractions around the square including museums and a huge statue of Chairman Mao is a popular attraction for taking selfies. The Imperial Mosque is to the west of the square, dating from the 16th century it is the largest mosque in the province of Sichuan. There are also several shopping malls close to the square.

36. Sichuan Museum of Science and Technology

This museum contains 20 permanent exhibition areas and can be found opposite Tianfu Square to the north and is located behind the giant statue of Mao Zedong (Chairman Mao). The first floor consists mainly of working models of key Sichuan technological development, a 4D theatre and exhibition halls for temporary exhibits. The second floor is devoted to machinery and one of the most interesting displays is a treadmill and how you can compete virtually against a range of animals. The fourth floor will have the interest of children with several interactive displays for younger children through to teenagers and beyond. The museum is closed on Monday's; it opens at 9am until 5pm on other days. It is free to enter but you need to show your passport.

37. Wangjiang Pavilion Park

This park is located on the Jinjiang Rivers south bank in the city. This park is dedicated to a female poet, Xue Tao who lived during the Tang Dynasty of 618-907. The park is full of bamboo with over 150 kinds growing here. The focal point of the park is the 'River Watching Tower' built in 1889 to honour the poet. It is free to visit the park, although a fee of CNY20 is charged to visit the historical relics on show. The park is open daily from 6am until 9pm.

38. Wenshu Monastery

This is one of my favourite attractions in Chengdu for the areas of peace and quiet that you can find here. It is located on Wenshu Yuan Street a little way to the north of Tianfu Square. It is the best preserved of Chengdu's Buddhist temples. It was originally built during the Tang dynasty of 618-907 and was at first called XinXiang Temple. Some of the highlights here include the collection of over 500 pieces of art in the form of calligraphy and paintings. A highly treasured item is the delicate Buddha made of Jade brought to China from Burma in 1922 by Xing Lin a Buddhist monk who walked the entire journey. There are more than 300 Buddha statues on display across the temple and gardens. The easiest way to get to Wenshu Monastery is the metro. On line 1 there is a station called Wenshuyuan or Wenshu Monastery. It is free to enter (in the past you had to pay a small fee) and is open daily from 8.30am until 5.30pm.

39. Wide and Narrow Alley

This is one of Chengdu's cultural and historical heritage centre's that has been preserved as a permanent reminder to the city's past. The area is actually three parallel alleys, Wide Alley, Narrow Alley and Well Alley in addition to 45 courtyards. The history of this area goes back to the Qing Dynasty of 1644-1911, at the time the area was full of quarters for troops stationed within the city. Once the troops left the area was neglected and left to decay. In 2003 renovation work began and the area was opened to the public in 2008 as a centre for tourism and recreation. The area today is a popular venue for restaurants, pubs, teahouses and stores.

You can visit this attraction on the metro, take line 4 to the Wide and Narrow Alley Station or line 2 to the People's Park station and walk along Upper Changshun Road.

40. Wuhou Temple

This temple is also known as the Memorial Temple of Marquis Wu. Zhuge Liang was the Marquis of Wu (Wuhou) during the Three Kingdoms Period 220-280AD. It can be found in the south of the city, is is unknown when it was originally built, the current temple was rebuilt in 1672. It is divided into 5 areas, the gate, the inner gate, the hall of Liu Bei, the corridor and the hall of Zhuge Liang. You can visit the temple via line 3 of Chengdu metro. Exit from the Gaoshengqiao station and walk along Wuhouci Avenue until you find the temple. The entry fee is CNY60 and it is open from 8am until 8pm. you should allow at least an hour for your visit.

41. Xiling Snow Mountain

Xiling Snow Mountain is 95km from Chengdu, it is a natural habitat for giant pandas and the 375 square kilometers make it a great location for skiing. The mountain top is snow covered all year and at 5346 metres high it is the tallest peak in the Chengdu area. The front of the mountain is ideal for hiking and a hike to the top of around 18km will take between 9 and 12 hours to complete. The back of the mountain is where you will find the best areas for skiing. This mountain is a popular resort all year, with plenty of summer activities including grass skiing. The ski resort has the longest cable car line in China; it takes 40 minutes to reach the top. You can snow ski here from December until late March. There are several buses each day that travel from Chengdu to Xiling Snow Mountain with most departures in the morning.

42. Yongling Museum

This museum is located on Yongling Road in the centre of Chengdu, it is built on the foundations of the Yongling Mausoleum the only above ground tomb known to have existed in China. It is also known as the Tomb of Wang Jian who lived from 847 until 918AD, he was the founder of the Shu Regime in a chaotic period of history after the fall of the Tang dynasty. The Yongling Mausoleum is circular in shape and has a diameter of 80 metres. It stands 15 metres high and has 14 archways. It was first excavated in 1942 by archaeologists.

Yongling Exhibition Hall is a modern building to the north of the mausoleum and houses relics from the tomb and other items from the Shu period. It is located in Yongling Park and even if you are not visiting for the historical or cultural experience then the park is a great setting for having a relaxing walk. The park and museum can be reached on metro line 4 at Kuanzhai Xiangzi station and leave by exit D; it is then a 1km walk to the north. Entry to the museum costs CNY20, the park is free. The museum is open daily from 8.30am until 6pm, the park from 6.30am until 10pm.

43. Zhaojue Temple

    This temple is next to the Chengdu Zoo in the north of the city. It is one of Sichuan's most famous temples and was the first Buddhist Monastery in the west of Sichuan. It was first built in the Tang dynasty of 618 until 907; it was destroyed during a battle in 1644 and rebuilt in 1663. To visit this temple take metro line 3 to the Chengdu Zoo station and the temple is just a 5 minute walk away. It costs just CNY2 and is open daily from 8am until 5pm.

44. Leshan Giant Buddha

    The Leshan Giant Buddha sits to the east of Leshan city in Sichuan province. It is located on a steep sided cliff at the confluence of three rivers, the Min, the Qingyi and the Dadu. It was included on the UNESCO list of World Heritage sites in 1996. It took thousands of workers 90 years to create, beginning in the year713 during the Tang dynasty. It is the world's biggest carved stone Buddha.

    It is 71 metres high, each finger is 8.3 metres long and the instep at 9 metres wide is big enough to contain more than one hundred people. The shoulders are 24 metres wide. A monk called Hai Tong began the project; the river had long been a cause for concern with the turbulent waters causing several boating tragedies. So the monk began his project believing the presence of such a deity would calm the waters. When Hai Tong died the project was less than half completed but two of his disciples continued with supervising the work.

    To visit here you can take a high speed train to Leshan from Chengdu than bus number 3 to the site. A good way to view the Giant

Buddha is from the river, there are several ferry companies operating from Leshan city. Entry to the site costs CNY90 and it is open daily from 9am until 4.30pm. It is advisable to avoid visiting on a national holiday as the lines of people waiting to see the Giant Buddha can take several hours.

45. Mount Emei

This famous peak among the mountains of southern Sichuan overlooks the city of Leshan, it towers above the city, is a sight of beauty, and is old and mysterious. On the mountain there are four scenic areas, the Baoguo Temple, the Wannian Temple the Qingyin Pavilion and the Golden Summit. The Golden Summit stands the highest at more than 3000 metres above sea level. As you ascend your way up the mountain you will observe some wonderful scenery such as waterfalls.

The mountain has a long history with people living here as long ago as 5000 years. The first monastery was built here more than 1900 years ago and the mountain has been connected to Buddhism since that time. Ticket prices vary between high and low season (December and January) from CNY110-185, with additional fees to see some attractions. You can use the ticket for more than one day if you stay overnight inside the park area. It opens daily from 6am until 6.30pm. 7am until 3.30 pm in the low season. You should take care when approached by monkeys in the park; they will snatch food from you if offered. Keep your food safely inside your bag.

46. Jiayang Steam Train

This is the only surviving steam train still operating in China in the mountainous and remote mining area close to Leshan in Sichuan province. While other train routes have been updated the route taken by the Jiayang Steam Train is still in operation. It used to be used for delivering coal and supplies for the Jiayang Coal Mine. Once the coal mine closed the train was kept in service as it was an important means of transportation for residents in the area.

The line is less than 20km long with 8 stops along its route. The train operates with signals using flags and whistles; there is no electrification on the train. Each carriage is fitted with a manual brake and telephones are old style. Students take the train to school; produce is loaded onto the carriages for market, even live animals.

There are three trains each day and it can become very crowded, particularly on market day or holidays. You find a seat and buy your ticket on the train, it costs CNY1 for one stop or CNY5 to take the whole route from Shixi to Huangcun Mine. There is a special sightseeing train each day, the seats are more comfortable but the train costs more, CNY100 for a round trip ticket. It runs at 10.30am each week day and at 1pm on the weekends.

There is one bus that goes direct from Chengdu to Jiayang each day, it departs at 9am and costs CNY70. Alternatives are to take a bus to Jianwei and then another to Jiayang, these buses run frequently.

>TOURIST

47. Sichuan Opera

The Sichuan Opera is a popular form of entertainment not just in Chengdu but also as far away as the provinces of Guizhou and Yunnan. The Sichuan Opera began during the Qing dynasty of 1644 until 1911, it brought together five different styles from other regions and they combined were the creation that is today's Sichuan opera. Changing faces is a famous local style and is best viewed in the Sichuan Opera Theatre on Zhuangyuan Street. Other notable locations for seeing this style of opera are Shunxing Old Tea House at the International Exhibition Centre, Shufeng Square in the People's Park or at Shufeng Yayun Garden in the Culture Park.

48. Shopping

The best area for shopping in Chengdu is around the huge shopping malls that all seem to converge along Chunxi Road, Luomashi and Zongfu Road. Here you can find just about everything you will ever need from tiny stalls to huge supermarkets. Chunxi Road has been an important commercial centre in Chengdu for more than 70 years. It is located just to the east of Tianfu Square and easy to reach on the metro lines 1 and 2.

49. Anshun Bridge

The Anshun Bridge is also known as the Dongman or East Gate Bridge across the Jinjiang River at Binjiang Road is a famous site in the centre of Chengdu. It is particularly impressive when lit up at night. It makes for an impressive backdrop when taking an evening stroll along the river.

50. Wenshufang Folk and Culture Street

The reconstructed area of this neighbourhood close to the Wenshu Monastery is a wonderful place to stroll and observe the local crafts on display in the tiny stores. There are several small restaurants in the area, stalls selling embroidered silks, jewelry stores with jade, gold and silver. So much to see and do.

Three Reasons To Book A Trip To Chengdu

Poetry- there are so many attractions here that have connections to ancient poets and to see how much they are revered today is quite staggering.

Monastery's And Ancient Temples- there are so many ancient places of worship to be found in and around Chengdu, so much history here to learn from.

Historical Ancient Towns- there are just so many historical attractions not too far from the centre of Chengdu to see how people lived hundreds of years ago.

> TOURIST
GREATER THAN A TOURIST

Visit GreaterThanATourist.com:
http://GreaterThanATourist.com

Sign up for the Greater Than a Tourist Newsletter:
http://eepurl.com/cxspyf

Follow us on Facebook:
https://www.facebook.com/GreaterThanATourist

Follow us on Pinterest:
http://pinterest.com/GreaterThanATourist

Follow us on Instagram:
http://Instagram.com/GreaterThanATourist

Follow on Twitter:
http://twitter.com/ThanaTourist

John Smither

> TOURIST
GREATER THAN A TOURIST

Please leave your honest review of this book on Amazon and Goodreads. Thank you. We appreciate your positive and constructive feedback. Thank you.

John Smither

NOTES

Made in the USA
Middletown, DE
20 December 2019